THE GERMAN COOKBOOK

DISCOVER THE BEST RECIPES FROM GERMANY

SARAH MILLER

CONTENTS

INTRODUCTION

Liebe Geht Durch den Magen or love goes through the stomach, isn't it true? Food is an emotion. It can bring together the people, the families, and the nations. Learning to cook Multi-Cuisines will not only add to your skills as a cook but will also help you understand different people and their cultures.

This Cookbook will not only help you learn to cook German food but will also increase your curiosity for the German Culture. It has some easy and authentic German recipes with detailed steps to guide you. Along with amazing taste, these recipes are also a treat for your eyes. The presentation and their unique shapes and easy methods will fill your heart with culinary joy and leave you with an everlasting taste.

So, if you are a fan of German food or wish to try it, we are here to help you! Making recipes from this book will allow you to enjoy the process of cooking as well as eating them.

Now, follow your heart and explore your Food world!

Alles Gute!

1. The Scrumptious Traditional German Schnitzel

T his Scrumptious recipe is a traditional and world-famous German dish. Various versions of Schnitzel exist across Germany. You can cook it with pork, chicken, or veal; it will taste equally delicious with any of these. Served with lemon slices or potatoes, it will leave you with everlasting culinary joy. So, let us see how to make this delicious dish.

Serving Size: 4

Preparation Time: 10 Minutes

Cooking Time: 6 Minutes

Ingredients:

- 4 Pork Chops or Steaks, Boneless
- ½ Cup All-purpose Flour
- ¾ Cup Breadcrumbs
- 2 Eggs, beaten
- Salt to taste,
- Pepper to taste

Instructions:

1. Mix a teaspoon of salt in the flour and set aside.

2. Throb the pork steaks on baking sheets until ¼ inches thick. Then, sprinkle some salt and pepper on both sides and set aside.

3. Take three bowls, add flour in one bowl, breadcrumbs in second, and beaten eggs in the third bowl.

4. Now, gently and lightly dip each pork chop, first, in the flour, then in the eggs, and finally in the crumbs. Make sure you coat all sides of pork, and crumbs do not press into the chops. Remove excess by shaking the chops.

5. Preheat a saucepan and fill it with enough oil that will allow the pork to swim in it.

6. When the oil reaches to 330°F, add the meat chops. Cook the chops for two to three minutes. Flip the chops once and cook another side for two-three minutes or until golden brown.

7. Serve hot with lemon and the sauce you desire, devour!

2. The Classic German Sauerbraten

Sauerbraten is considered as a national food of Germany. Marinating meat with various ingredients for one or two hours and then cooking is a specialty of this traditional dish. It is a perfect blend of health and taste. You can have it with a sweet sauce or spätzle for an even better experience. Let us go through the steps of making this devouring dish.

Serving Size: 4

Preparation Time: 25 Minutes

Cooking Time: 3 hours

Ingredients:

- 4 lb. beef chuck roast, boneless
- 4 Cups Water
- 2 Cups Red Wine Vinegar
- ¼ Cup All-Purpose Flour
- 12 Cloves
- 5 Carrots, cut into 1-inch pieces
- 2 Celery ribs, cut into 1-inch pieces
- 1 Onion, sliced
- 2 Bay Leaves
- 2 tbsp Canola Oil

- 3 tsp Brown Sugar
- 3 tsp Salt

Instructions:

1. In a bowl, pour in the water and add brown sugar, Cloves, Bay Leaves, Red wine vinegar, and salt. Combine and transfer two cups of the mixture to a small bowl. Cover the small bowl and refrigerate for a day or two.

2. Now, add the remaining mixture to a resealable plastic bag, add the beef chuck roast, seal the bag, and set aside to refrigerate for a day or two. While refrigerating, turn it twice on each day.

3. Remove the spices and the marinade.

4. Pat the dry roast and dip it in flour to coat all the sides.

5. In a large skillet, heat oil and keep the flame medium-high. Add the roast and fry until brown on all sides.

6. Transfer the roast to a roasting pan and add the onion, carrot, and the celery to it.

7. Now, pour in the marinade from the small bowl.

8. Transfer to the oven and bake for about three and a half hours until the meat is tender over 325°Fahrenheit.

9. Serve hot and devour!

3. Creamy and Classy Potato Soup

Germany is known for its varieties and taste of Potatoes. This Classy potato soup will feed your cravings for German food and help you keep your winter nights warm and healthy. The soup has a delicious taste of potatoes, vegetables, bacon, and it tastes exponentially delicious when you add the special wiener Sausages to it. It is so delicious that you will want to have it twice or even thrice. Let us discuss these easy steps of making it.

Serving Size: 4
Preparation Time: 10 minutes
Cooking Time: 30 Minutes
Ingredients:

- 1 1/3 lb. mealy potatoes, peeled and diced
- 7 oz Carrots, chopped
- 3 ½ oz Streaky Bacon, diced
- 4 Cups Vegetable Stock
- 4 Wiener Sausages, sliced
- 1 Onion, chopped
- 4 tsp Oil
- 1/3 tsp Caraway

5

- 1/3 tsp Marjoram
- 1 Leek, sliced
- 1 Parsley root, chopped
- 1 Bay leave
- ½ celery root, chopped
- Nutmeg

Instructions:

1. Heat a pan with oil and add the diced bacon to it. Then add the chopped onions and sauté.

2. Mix the vegetables and simmer for ten minutes.

3. Add the Vegetable stock, Caraway and marjoram, and cook for thirty minutes.

4. Now, remove the one-third of the vegetable greens and set aside in a pot.

5. Smash the rest of the greens for thickness.

6. Add the diced Vegetables. Season your soup with Ground pepper.

7. Now, add the sausages and let them simmer.

8. Serve with Parsley.

4. Flavourful Sausage and Egg Burrito for Breakfast

The Breakfast of Sausage and Burrito will provide you essential proteins and keep you energetic the whole day. You can make this breakfast more delicious if you serve it in the form of a Burrito. They are easy to make and also to eat. You can easily make them in the rush hours of the morning in less time and start your day on a healthy note.

Serving Size: 6
Preparation Time: 5 Minutes
Cooking Time: 25 Minutes
Ingredients:

- 1 lb. Sausages
- 6 Eggs
- 6 Flour Tortillas
- 1 Can diced Tomatoes
- 1 Cup Cheddar Cheese
- ½ Cup Yellow Onion, Chopped
- 3 tbsp Milk, Reduced Fat
- ¼ tsp Salt
- 1/8 tsp Pepper

Instructions:

1. In a mixing bowl, blend eggs, salt, milk, and pepper. Set aside until needed.

2. Heat a skillet over medium-high heat and cook sausages for about five minutes.

3. Add the onions and diced tomatoes and cook further for about two minutes until the onions are tender and sausages no longer pink. Now strain and transfer the mixture to a pot.

4. Now, add the egg mixture to the same skillet. As soon as the edges begin to set, turn the eggs to scramble and cook until eggs almost cook.

5. Now, place a half cup of the meat mixture into a tortilla. Fill the rest of the tortilla with an equal amount of cheese and the eggs.

6. Fold two opposite sides and roll it.

7. Follow the same steps for other Burritos and cut each into half.

8. Devour!

5. The Easter Bread

The Easter Bread is a traditional German bread eaten during or on Easter mornings for breakfast. There are various varieties of Easter bread, depending upon the cities. This fancy and delicious bread is easy to make with only a few ingredients. You can enjoy it for breakfast with your family. Let me share with you the steps of making this traditional bread.

Serving Size: 5

Preparation Time: 2 Hours

Cooking Time: 35 Minutes

Ingredients:

- 1¼ lb. All-Purpose Flour
- 8 ½ oz Cream
- 1¾ oz Sugar
- 1 tbsp Milk
- 1 tsp vanilla extract
- 2 Eggs
- 1 Egg white
- 1 Yolk
- 1 Envelope rapid Yeast

Instructions:

1. Take a large bowl and combine flour and sugar.

2. Add 3 1/3 oz of the cream to a bowl and place it in the oven for a short period until it is Luke warm and then sprinkle some yeast on it. Set aside for five minutes.

3. Now, add the eggs and an egg white to the flour mixture.

4. Add the yeast and cream mixture to the flour mixture.

5. Now Lukewarm the remaining cream and add it to the flour mixture. Whisk until sticky dough forms.

6. Now, knead the dough on a lightly floured surface and shape into a bowl.

7. Place the dough into a bowl, cover with a towel, and set aside for around forty-five minutes.

8. Preheat your oven to 350°Fahrenheit.

9. Take the dough out and divide it into three equal portions and make balls.

10. Shape each bowl into a strand. Keep these strands

next to each other, leaving some space in between.

11. Now, start braiding from middle to one end and again from the mid to another end.

12. Develop a circle of braid and tuck the last strand under the other. Now, set it aside for fifteen minutes covered with a towel.

13. In a bowl, add the yolk and a tablespoon of milk. Mix well.

14. Now, apply this mixture to the bread using a brush.

15. Place your Easter bread into the oven and bake for twenty to thirty minutes or until light brown.

16. Let it cool a bit and Enjoy your Easter bread while it's still a little warm.

6. Oktoberfest Special Glühwine

Glühwine is a traditional German drink that is usually made with red wine. Unlike other drinks, this Glühwine includes spices like cinnamon, cloves, star anise, etc. It helps in keeping you warm, and its recommended to drink it while it is still warm. Now, let us see the steps of making it.

Serving Size: 8

Preparation Time: 5 Minutes

Cooking Time: 15 Minute

Ingredients:

- 1 ½ bottle Cabernet Sauvignon
- 2 Cups Water
- 1 ½ Cups Sugar
- 1 Cup orange juice
- 2 Oranges, cut into halves
- 1 Lemon, cut into halves
- 10 Cloves
- 8 Allspice Berries
- 8 Juniper Berries
- 3 Cinnamon Sticks
- 1 Star Anise
- Orange twists

Instructions:

1. Heat a pot over high heat and add the water, orange juice 2 Cinnamon sticks, star anise, sugar, and allspice berries.

2. Bring the mixture to boil over high heat. Then reduced the heat and let the mixture simmer.

3. Now, squeeze the halved oranges into the mixture for juice. Add cloves into its rinds, and gently add it into the pot.

4. Now, add the juniper berries.

5. Squeeze the lemons in the boiling mixture and gently add its rinds as well.

6. Heat the juice until it reduces to half of its actual amount and then add the cabernet sauvignon to it. Heat until about to simmer.

7. Pour into your glasses or mugs and serve hot with the remaining cinnamon stick and an orange twist.

7. German Potato Salad

There are different types of potatoes and potato salad in Germany. This delicious potato salad is mostly found in southern Germany and is served warm, unlike other Salads. The extra delicious combination of Potatoes and Bacon dressed with a tangy taste of Vinegar is a perfect side dish for your barbeque lunch. Now, let us go through the quick and easy steps of making it.

Serving Size: 6
Preparation Time: 10 Minutes
Cooking Time: 30 Minutes
Ingredients:

- 2 lb. Red Potatoes
- 6 Bacon slices, chopped
- 2 Cups Onions, finely chopped
- ½ Cup Chicken broth
- ½ Cup Parsley, finely Chopped
- ¼ Cup apple cider Vinegar

- 2 tbsp Olive oil
- 1tbsp Dijon Mustard
- 2 tsp Sugar, granulated
- ½ tsp Garlic, Chopped
- Salt to taste

Pepper to taste

Instructions:

1. In a steaming basket, add the potatoes. Now, place the basket in a pot filled with one and a half inches of water. Now, bring the potatoes to boil over a medium-high flame. (If you do not have a steaming basket, boil directly in the water, by adding a tablespoon of salt in it.)

2. Now, cover the pot with a lid and let it simmer for about twenty minutes or until the potatoes are tender. Set aside to cool.

3. Meanwhile, in a skillet, add the bacon and cook for about six minutes.

4. When slices of bacon look crispy, transfer them to another bowl. Leave the dripped fat in the skillet itself.

5. Now, add the onions in the same skillet and cook it with the drippings. Cook the Onions about 5 minutes and then add the garlic and cook for another 30 Seconds.

6. Now, add the Dijon mustard, apple cider vinegar, chicken broth, and sugar to the mixture and bring it to boil. Simmer for about two minutes until it reduces to half of its actual volume.

7. Now, chop the boiled potatoes and add them to the mixture.

8. Add the bacon, olive oil, salt, and pepper to taste.

9. If the salad looks dry, add a bit of chicken broth. If it looks as desired, remove from heat and garnish with Parsley.

10. Serve hot!

8. Hopple Popple Casserole for Breakfast

Hopple Popple Casserole is made with various vegetables, eggs, and available meat. This breakfast rich in nutrients is a good source of Calcium. It is simple to make and does not require any special efforts to make it. You can also utilize the leftovers from the previous day to make it and also have it for lunch or supper. So, let see how to make this multipurpose traditional Hopple Popple Casserole.

Serving Size: 6

Preparation Time: 10 Minutes

Cooking Time: 15 Minutes

Ingredients:

- 5-6 Eggs
- 3-4 Cups Brown hash potatoes
- 1 Cup cheddar cheese, shredded
- 1 Cup Mozzarella Cheese, shredded
- ½ cup Milk

- 1/3 cup Onions, chopped
- 25 Pepperoni slices
- 4 tbsp butter, divided
- ½ tsp salt
- ½ tsp butter
- Mix herbs

Instructions:

1. Cover a half-inch of a heated pan with potatoes and add butter and onions to it. Cook until light brown. Now, spread the mixture in the pan, evenly.

2. In a bowl, add the seasonings, milk, and eggs. Mix well and pour it over the pan mixture.

3. Arrange pepperoni on top of it.

4. Cover the pan with a lid and cook for about ten minutes or until the eggs set.

5. Now, remove the lid from the pan and sprinkle the shredded cheese on top.

6. Now, place the lid back on the pan and let cook for about two to three minutes.

7. Cut into wedges and serve hot with toasts.

9. The German Vacation Cocktail

This drink is so delicious that just a sip of it will take you to German beaches and the sunbath, sitting at your home. It is an interesting blend of aged rum and Jägermeister and addition of orgeat, fresh lemon juice, and Peychaud's bitter makeup for an everlasting taste. If you have all ingredients ready, it will take only a few minutes to make it. Now, let us go through the steps of making this Amazing German Vacation Cocktail.

Serving Size: 1
Preparation Time: 3 Minutes
Ingredients:

- 1 oz Jägermeister
- 1 oz gold rum, Flor de Cana 4 years
- ¾ oz Domaine de Cantone
- ¾ oz orgeat
- ¾ oz Fresh lemon juice
- 3 Dash Peychaud's bitter

Instructions:

1. Fill a blender with ice and add Jägermeister, rum, Domaine de Cantone, orgeat, and fresh lemon juice.

2. Shake well to combine.

3. Now, add ice in your glass and strain the cocktail in it.

4. Mound the ice on top of it like a cone.

5. Now, top the glass with three dashes of Peychaud's bitter.

6. Serve!

10. Schwartzwälder Kirschtorte AKA Black Forest Cherry Cake

There is a mountainous region in Germany called "schwartzwälder" or the Black Forest. "Kirschwasser" or the Cherry liquor, the famous ingredient used in this Black Forest cake, is found in this region, thus the name Black Forest Cherry Cake. The heavenly presentation of this cake itself is enough to make your mouth water. It will not take more than a few minutes to finish this delicious cake once you taste it. Now, let us go through the steps of making this delectable cake.

Serving Size: 8
Preparation Time: 30 Minutes
Cooking Time: 40 Minutes
Ingredients:

- 1 Box Dark Chocolate Cake mix
- 21 Oz Cherry Pie Filling
- 1 ½ Oz semisweet Chocolate
- 1 Container Whipped Icing
- 3 Cups Heavy Cream
- 1/3 cup Confectioners' Sugar
- ¼ Cup Cherry brandy, divided

- 1 tsp Red Food Color
- 1 tsp Vanilla Extract
- Few Maraschino Cherries

Instructions:

1. Following the instructions on the cake box, bake two cakes in 9-inch cake pans. Add the food color and vanilla extract as instructed. When both cakes bake, allow them to cool on a cooling rack.

2. Now, wrap the cakes in a plastic wrap and refrigerate for about an hour.

3. Meanwhile, in a mixing bowl, add the confectioner's sugar and whipped cream. Blend well and refrigerate.

4. Now, take the cakes out and cut both cakes in half, horizontally, to make a total of four layers.

5. On a plate, place the first layer of the cake and brush it with cherry brandy (2 tbsp).

6. Fill a pastry bag with icing and make a circle around the edges of the first layer. Now, Spread the pie filling within this circle.

7. Follow the same steps for the second and third layers.

8. Now, add the fourth layer and frost the whole cake with the whipped cream.

9. Now, arrange the Maraschino Cherries on top of the cake.

10. Using a peeler, shave the semisweet chocolate to curl cup-like wooden shavings.

11. Sprinkle the chocolate shaves on the top and press on the sides of the cake.

12. Refrigerate for two hours.

13. Enjoy!

11. Hearty German Coleslaw

This German Coleslaw is about to become your favorite. This traditional German recipe is oozing in nutrition. It is mainly cabbage-based, and the bacon and tangy dressing of the vinegar adds flavors to it. It is simple to make but delicious enough to make it to your party menu. So, let us see how to make this hearty dish.

Serving Size: 4
Preparation Time: 10 Minutes
Ingredients:

- 8 Cups Cabbage, chopped
- 4 Cups Carrots, chopped
- ½ Cup Red Onions, finely chopped
- ½ Cup Vegetable Oil
- ½ Cup Vinegar
- 1/3 Cup Sugar
- ¼ Cup Bacon bits
- 1 ½ tsp Salt

Instructions:

1. In a large bowl, add the cabbage, carrots, onions, and the bacon bits and mix well until combine.

2. Now, in another medium bowl, add all the remaining ingredients to it. Mix well.

3. Now, add this mixture to the cabbage mixture and mix until well combined.

4. Now, place the bowl in the refrigerator to chill for about an hour.

5. Serve!

12. Creamy and Tasty Senfeier

Senfeier, made with boiled eggs and homemade mustard sauce, is the children's favorite dish. If you want your kids to eat healthily, this Senfeier is a perfect choice. It is simple, healthy, and delicious. Also, it does not require much effort to cook. So, let us go through a few easy steps of making this flavourful dish.

Serving Size: 8

Preparation Time: 5 Minutes

Cooking Time: 15 Minutes

Ingredients:

- 25 oz vegetable broth
- 2¼ oz Flour
- 8 Eggs, boiled
- ½ Cup Onions, diced
- 2 tbsp Mustard
- 2 tbsp Margarine
- 1 Pinch sugar
- Salt to taste

Instructions:

1. In a saucepan, fry the onions and margarine.

2. Then add the flour, vegetable broth, and the salt and cook for about fifteen minutes.

3. Season with mustard and sugar.

4. Now, on a plate, place the boiled eggs and pour the sauce over it.

5. Devour!

13. German Styled Potato Dumplings

This traditional but comforting dish is about to become your favorite. These potato dumplings made from boiled potatoes, eggs, and breadcrumbs are delectable with the browned butter sauce. These are soft and scrumptious and can be topped with bacon if you desire. You can also serve these dumplings as a side dish for gravy or roast or even sausages. So, let us see how to make this versatile dish.

Serving Size: 8
Preparation Time: 40 Minutes
Cooking Time: 10 Minutes
Ingredients:

- 3 lb. Potatoes, peeled and quartered
- 12 Cups Water
- 1 Cup All-Purpose Flour
- ½ Cup Butter
- 2/3 Cup Breadcrumbs, dry
- 3 Eggs, beaten
- 1 tbsp Onions, Chopped
- 1 tsp Salt
- ½ tsp ground nutmeg
- ¼ Cup Breadcrumbs

Instructions:

1. In a large pot, add the potatoes and the water just enough to cover the potatoes. Add salt to taste and bring potatoes to boil. Let simmer for about 15 minutes or until the potatoes are tender.

2. Now, drain and transfer the potatoes to a large bowl. Allow them to cool.

3. When cooled, mash the potatoes and add the flour, salt, eggs, nutmeg, and the 2/3 cup breadcrumbs.

4. Mix well to combine and then form sixteen balls out of the mixture.

5. Now, bring twelve cups of salted water in a pot or unsalted water in a Dutch oven to simmer.

6. Now, carefully add the dumplings to the water and cook for about ten minutes on a low flame.

7. Flip occasionally to cook entirely. Insert a toothpick in dumplings to check whether the dumplings have cooked.

8. To make the sauce, in a pan, add the butter and the onions. Stir continuously over medium flame until golden brown.

9. In a bowl, add ¼ Cup Breadcrumbs.

10. When butter is golden brown, remove the mixture from heat and transfer to the Bread crumb Bowl.

11. Now, stir the mixture in with breadcrumbs until combine.

12. Devour!

14. Colorful Dinner with Brats and Veggies

This Colorful and flavorful meal is a perfect dish for celebrating Oktoberfest or for Fall. It is easy to prepare with a few ingredients that are available in your kitchen. Brats are already delicious and adding roasted vegetables to it makes it more and more flavorful and delectable. You can serve it with pasta or sauerkraut for a fulfilling experience. So, let us see the steps for preparing a colorful dinner for you.

Serving Size: 4

Preparation Time: 10 Minutes

Cooking Time: 30 Minutes

Ingredients:

- 6 Potatoes, quartered
- 3 Bratwursts
- 1 Bunch asparagus, chopped into 2-inch pieces
- 1 Medium Onion, diced
- 1 Apple, diced
- 1 Red bell pepper, diced
- 3 tbsp cooking wine
- 3 tbsp balsamic vinegar
- Garlic salt
- Salt
- Pepper

Instructions:

1. In a pot, heat water or beer and add Bratwursts to it. Partly cook the bratwursts and slice into ½ inch circles. Set aside.

2. Partly cook potatoes as well.

3. In a large bowl, combine the onions, apple, asparagus, red bell pepper.

4. Now, add to it the pre-cooked potatoes and Bratwursts. Now, add the vinegar, olive oil, and the wine. Mix well or toss

until all ingredients are well coated. Set aside for a few minutes to marinate.

5. Now, heat the grill basket and grill and the mixture to it. Now, cover the basket with lid and cook for about five minutes, occasionally stirring and flipping to avoid burning.

6. When the veggies are tender, and brats have thoroughly cooked, transfer the veggies to a plate or serving bowl.

7. Serve immediately!

15. The Beloved Berliner Doughnut or Pfannkuchen

The Berliner is a world-famous jelly doughnut, and now, you can make it at your home. It is a traditional German doughnut without a central hole. It is mostly known as Pfannkuchen in Berlin. With sugar icing from outside, the doughnut is filled with delicious jam or jelly inside. Irresistible! Isn't it? So, let us quickly go through the steps of making this sweet treat for you!

Serving Size: 8
Preparation Time: 2 hours
Cooking Time: 20 Minutes
Ingredients:

- 3 oz Butter
- 3 cups All-Purpose Flour
- 1 1/3 cups granulated sugar
- 1 cup jam or jelly
- ¾ Cup Buttermilk
- 1 ½ tsp dry or instant yeast
- 1 tsp kosher salt
- ½ tsp vanilla extract
- ½ tsp ground cinnamon
- 2 Eggs

Instructions:

1. In a mixing bowl, add ½ Cup of lukewarm water and then add the yeast. Blend and set it aside for about five minutes to activate.

2. Now, add the flour, butter, buttermilk, eggs, salt, vanilla extract, and 1/3 cup granulated sugar to it. Blend in a mixing bowl attached with dough hook over low speed for a minute. Now, scrape down the sides of the bowl and blend again over high speed for about two minutes.

3. Now, spray a large bowl with non-stick spray and place the dough in it. Cover the dough with plastic wrap and refrigerate for about two hours or until the dough doubles in its volume.

4. Meanwhile, in a bowl, add the remaining granulated sugar and the cinnamon. Mix well and set aside.

5. In a piping bag, add the jam or jelly and fit the bag with a narrow tip.

6. Now, prepare a baking sheet with a paper napkin and flour it lightly. Set aside.

7. Take the dough out from the refrigerator and roll it out on a lightly floured surface until its ¾ inches thick.

8. Using a 3½-inch cookie cutter, cut out 12 circles from the dough and place on the prepared baking sheet.

9. Now, in a large deep pot, add oil up to 3 inches and heat it until it reaches 350° Fahrenheit.

10. Carefully drop the donuts in batches and fry each side for about five minutes or until donuts are thoroughly fried.

11. Line a plate with paper towels and place the fried doughnuts on it. Use a slotted spoon to strain the oil. Set aside to cool.

12. When the donuts are a little warm, create a cavity using a back of a wooden spoon. First, create a hole from one side to three-quarters and then move the handle around to make room for jam.

13. Now, add the jam inside until the doughnut is a little heavy.

14. Repeat for all the doughnuts and place them on a large plate.

15. Sprinkle the sugar and cinnamon mixture.

16. Enjoy your own Berliner!

16. Flaky and Flavorsome Potato Gratin

A lot of German recipes are cooked with potatoes, yet they are so different in taste from one another that we cannot ever get bored of eating potatoes. In this recipe, potatoes are layered and cooked with cream and cheese and spiced up with salt and pepper. This delightful blend makes this recipe more flavorsome and flaky to eat. You can also add other herbs if you desire. Let me share with you the steps of making this delicious dish.

Serving Size: 8
Preparation Time: 20 Minutes
Cooking Time: 1 hour 30 Minutes
Ingredients:

- 6 lb. Potatoes, peeled and sliced 1/8 inch thick
- 2 ½ Cups Heavy Cream
- 2 Cups Cheese, grated
- 1 tsp Salt
- Ground Black Pepper to taste

Instructions:

1. Butter a 9-inch Pan and preheat your oven to 375° Fahrenheit.

2. Now, arrange the potato slices in a staggered row in the pan. While placing the potatoes, alternatively place slices of different potatoes.

3. When the pan is full, pour in the heavy cream and season with salt and pepper. Also, if you want to add any other herbs, this is the time.

4. Now, place the pan in the oven and bake for about an hour. Then, take it out and sprinkle the grated cheese on it.

Place it back in the oven and bake again until the potatoes are tender.

5. Enjoy!

17. German Potato Omelette

The German Potato Omelette is an easy and simple dish to serve over breakfast. This dish is prepared by cooking potatoes and onions and adding them to the eggs and milk mixture. It is simple and fulfilling. You can also modify it by adding cheese while the omelet is cooking. Serve it hot with some pickle, jam, or toast and season as per your choice for a desirable taste. Now, let us discuss the steps of making it.

Serving Size: 4
Preparation Time: 10 Minutes
Cooking Time: 20 Minutes
Ingredients:

- 8 Eggs
- 2 Potatoes, finely sliced
- ½ Cup Onions, finely chopped
- ¼ Cup of milk
- ¼ Cup butter, divided

- Salt to taste
- Pepper to taste

Instructions:

1. Heat a skillet and add to it 2 tbsp of butter and sliced potatoes. Cook for about fifteen minutes until potatoes are tender.

2. Now, add the onions and then set aside for a while.

3. Take a bowl and add the eggs and butter. Whisk well to combine.

4. Now, heat a skillet over a medium-high flame, add the remaining butter and then the eggs and milk mixture.

5. As eggs set, place the potatoes on one side of the egg and fold it with the other side.

6. Now, season it as you desire, cut, and serve!

18. The Refreshing Apple Cider Cocktail

This refreshing Apple cider cocktail is a perfect drink for your fall party. It's refreshing taste and simplicity will rejuvenate all your guests. Also, you do not need to prepare for it way before your guests arrive. It is simple to make and does not require a lot of ingredients. So, let us go through a few easy steps of making this refreshing drink.

Serving Size: 1

Preparation Time: 2 Minutes

Ingredients:

- 3 oz Apple cider
- 2 oz Ginger beer
- 2 oz bourbon
- ½ tsp lime juice
- Apple slice
- Cinnamon stick

Instructions:

1. Fill a shake with ice and add into it the apple cider, lemon juice, and bourbon. Shake the mixture well for about a half minute.

2. Strain the mixture into an ice-filled glass.

3. Now, add the ginger beer to it.

4. Garnish with a slice of apple and cinnamon stick.

5. Serve!

19. The Farmer's Breakfast

The Farmer's Breakfast is a fulfilling dish made with various ingredients like roasted potatoes, eggs, bacon, etc. Although it is called breakfast, you can also eat it as lunch or dinner. It is a hearty dish that you can prepare in less time. It is so delicious that you will make it again and again. So, let us see the steps of making this hearty dish.

Serving Size: 4
Preparation Time: 10 Minutes
Cooking Time: 15 Minutes
Ingredients:

- 4 Eggs, beaten
- 3 Potatoes, quartered
- 2 Cups Bell Pepper, Chopped
- 2 Cups Onions, chopped
- 1-2 cups ham, chopped
- ¼ Cup parsley, chopped
- 3 tbsp, bacon fat
- Salt to taste
- Pepper to taste

Instructions:

1. In a pot, heat water, add a little salt, and boil potatoes for about fifteen minutes or until the potatoes are slightly underdone.

2. When done, drain the potatoes and allow to cool a bit.

3. Cut into same-size squares.

4. Now, heat a saucepan with the two tablespoons of bacon fat and add chopped onions and red bell pepper. Stir until brown for about two to three minutes.

5. Now, push onions and pepper to the edges and add the potatoes and a tablespoon of fat.

6. Cook for few minutes until browned.

7. Season with salt and pepper.

8. Now, frequently stirring, add the ham and cook for about two minutes until hams cook through. Stir until all veggies are mixed.

9. Add the parsley to the mixture and stir again to combine.

10. Add the beaten eggs to the mixture and stir to mix eggs with the veggies and ham.

11. As the eggs begin to set, remove the mixture from heat and transfer to plate.

12. Serve with ketchup!

20. The German Egg Noodles

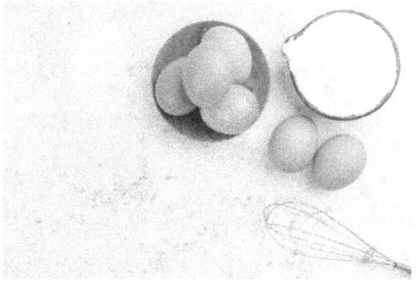

There couldn't be a delicious way to be healthy than including eggs for your daily meal. Also, Eggs are great to experiment with as nothing ever goes wrong with the eggs. And this German-style egg noodles are now going to make it to your list of delicious experiments. Popularly known as Spätzle in Germany, this dish has a perfect texture and perfect taste. You can also store it for a few days, and they will still be equally fresh and delicious. Now, let me share with you the steps of making egg noodles.

Serving Size: 6

Preparation Time: 25 Minutes

Cooking Time: 10 Minutes

Ingredients:

- 4 Large Eggs
- 2 Cups All-Purpose Flour
- ½ Cup Milk, divided
- 1 ½ tbsp Salt
- Butter
- Water

Instructions:

1. In a standing mixer, add the flour and salt. Mix to combine.

2. In another bowl, beat eggs.

3. Now, push the flour to the edges in the mixture and add the eggs in it.

4. Add the milk to it as needed to make a dough. Place the dough hook to the mixer and knead it for about fifteen to twenty minutes. After kneading for about fifteen minutes, spoon some mixture using a wooden spoon. If bubbles appear, the dough is done.

5. In a pot, bring 2 quarts water to boil, allow it to simmer.

6. Now, add the mixture to the ricer or Spätzle maker and press it on the water.

7. Cook noodles for three minutes or until the noodles float to the top.

8. Fill a bowl with Ice water and transfer noodles to it as soon as noodles cook. Dump, drain and toss the noodles with butter.

9. Serve warm!

21. Classic German Fish Fry

Fish is one of the favorite food in Germany, and this German-style fish fry recipe will make it your favorite too. It makes a flaky and fulfilling dish. You can choose any fish you like and follow these steps to fry it, and it will not fail to devour you. Also, you do not have to be a chef to make it right. It is easy to cook with a few steps. Now, let us see how to make this classic dish.

Serving Size: 4
Preparation Time: 10 Minutes
Cooking Time: 10 Minutes
Ingredients:

- 4 Fish fillets
- 2 Eggs

- 1 Cup Flour
- 6 tbsp Breadcrumbs
- 1 Tbsp lemon juice
- Butter or oil
- Salt to taste

Instructions:

1. Splash some lemon juice on the fish and season it with salt.

2. Take three bowls, add beaten eggs in one, flour in second, and breadcrumbs in the third bowl.

3. Heat a pan over medium-high heat and add the butter to it.

4. Now, coat the fish fillets, first with the flour, then with the eggs, and finally with breadcrumbs.

5. Place the fish in the heated pan to fry. Flip once and fry until golden brown or cook through.

6. Devour!

22. Delicious Spaghetti Ice Cream

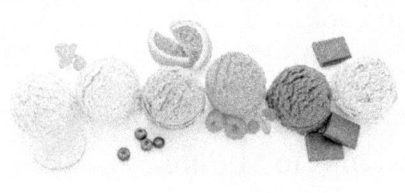

I know no one can ever get bored of Ice-Cream, but if a little experiment can make it exponentially delicious, who would not be willing to try. This spaghetti Ice-cream will please your eyes along with your taste buds. And you will be surprised to know that you do not need any extra-special ingredients to make it, just some Vanilla Ice-cream and strawberries. So, without wasting any more time, let us quickly go through the steps of making it.

Serving Size: 4
Preparation Time: 20 Minutes
Cooking Time: 5 Minutes
Ingredients:

- 8 oz Strawberries, quartered
- 1 Tbsp sugar
- 2 tsp orange juice
- Vanilla Ice-cream.
- White Chocolate Shavings.

Instructions:

1. Chill your Ice-Cream plates and potato ricer in the refrigerator.

2. In a food processor or a blender, add the quartered strawberries along with sugar and let stand for about five to ten minutes.

3. Now, add Orange juice and blend for about five minutes. Transfer it to the jar and place it in the refrigerator.

4. Take the potato ricer out and place the vanilla Ice-Cream into it. Now, press it to allow Ice-Cream noodles to fell into the plate.

5. Garnish with the strawberry mixture and white chocolate shavings.

6. Enjoy!

23. The Delicious German Strudels

This traditional German dish is a famous recipe served during Oktoberfest. Made with Pastry Puff, Bratwursts, a lot of cheese, and Caraway seeds, the taste of these strudels increases with each bite. It is savory and flavourful. Once tasted, you cannot wait to make it again. So, let us see how to make this savory dish.

Serving Size: 3
Preparation Time: 25 Minutes
Cooking Time: 30 Minutes
Ingredients:

- 5 Bratwurst links, cooked
- 1 Onion, chopped
- 17.3 oz frozen puff pastry, thawed
- 14 oz Sauerkraut, rinsed and drained
- 1 Cup Muenster Cheese, shredded
- 1 Cup Cheddar Cheese, shredded
- ½ cup sour cream
- 3 tbsp Dijon mustard
- 1 tbsp Butter

2 ½ tsp Caraway seeds

Instructions:

1. Preheat your oven to 400° Fahrenheit.

2. In a large pan, heat the butter over medium-high flame.

3. Now, add the onion and bratwurst links to it and cook for about ten minutes or until onions are tender.

4. Add the sauerkraut to it and stir to combine. Allow it to slightly cool.

5. Meanwhile, in a bowl, mix the mustard, sour cream and half teaspoon Caraway seeds.

6. Now, open a side of puff pastry and add the 1/3 cup of sour cream and spread it. Then add the 2 cups of sausage mixture in the center of pastry puff and sprinkle ½cup of each of the cheeses.

7. Now, to close the pastry puff, slightly brush its edges with water and bring them together and pinch. Place on a baking sheet, pinch the ends and brush the tops.

8. Sprinkle caraway seed on it and cut slits. Bake for about thirty minutes. Set aside for a few minutes.

9. Slice and serve!

24. The Classic German Burger

If you are a burger lover, this Classic German burger is ready to devour you! It is easy to make with burger buns and ground beef and some spices. Feel free to add more ingredients and more than one patty in a burger to double the fun. Now, let us proceed with the steps of making this Classic Burger.

Serving Size: 8
Preparation Time: 15 Minutes
Cooking Time: 20 Minutes
Ingredients:

- 2 lb. ground beef, lean
- 2 Onions, sliced
- 2 Eggs, beaten
- 1 Onion, minced
- 2 tbsp All-Purpose Flour
- 2 tbsp Parsley, chopped
- 2 tbsp butter
- ½ tsp Salt
- 1/8 tsp Nutmeg, ground

- 1/8 tsp Black Paper
- 8 Burger buns

Instructions:

1. In a bowl, add all-purpose flour, minced onion, salt, pepper, and nutmeg mix well and form 8 patties out of it.

2. In a large saucepan, heat butter and fry the patties until golden brown.

3. Now, transfer the patties from the pan to a plate or tray and fry onions in the drippings.

4. Place a patty in a burger, top with sliced onions, parsley, lettuce, tomato, or any other ingredients you desire.

5. Devour!

25. Succulent Sweet German Dumplings with Vanilla Sauce

Dumplings with Vanilla Sauce is a traditional and popular sweet dish in Germany. It includes dumplings made with sugar and milk cooked in poaching liquid. It is a delicious dish and tastes even better when served with Vanilla sauce. You can serve it as a sweet dish at any party and see the excitement level rising. It will not only give you a culinary joy but will also make you famous among your peers. So, let me share the steps of making this delicious dish.

Serving Size: 8

Preparation Time: 30 Minutes

Cooking Time: 50 Minutes

Ingredients:

For the dumplings

- 14¼ oz All-Purpose Flour
- 3¾ oz Milk
- 3 1/3 oz Baker's Sugar
- 2½ oz Unsalted Butter, melted
- ½ tbsp instant yeast
- 1Egg, beaten

For Vanilla Sauce

- 4¾ oz Milk
- 4 Egg yolks
- 2½ oz Sugar
- 1 Vanilla pod (seeds)

For Poaching Liquid

- 1½ oz Milk
- 1¾ Butter
- 1¾ sugar

Instructions:

1. For the dumplings, mix the yeast and a teaspoon of

sugar in lukewarm water. Stand aside for five to ten minutes until the bubbles appear. You can proceed if the bubbles appear. Make sure to use only lukewarm water for this, or yeast will go waste.

2. Now, in a large bowl, add the remaining sugar, flour, and butter. Add the yeast mixture to it. Combine well and then knead the dough using your hands on a lightly floured surface until smooth and springy dough forms.

3. Transfer the dough in an already greased bowl and cover it with a plastic wrap. Set aside for about an hour or until doubled in volume.

4. Meanwhile, in a pan, warm the vanilla seeds and milk to make the vanilla sauce.

5. In a bowl, mix the sugar and egg yolk. Now, pour in the vanilla seeds and milk mixture on it.

6. Mix it well and then transfer back to the pan. Stir continuously over low flame for about twenty minutes or until thick.

7. When the dough is almost prepared, start with the poaching liquid. To make this, add the milk, butter, and sugar in a large saucepan and heat until the sugar and butter melt.

8. Now, divide the dough into eight equal portions and form small balls.

9. Dump and place the balls into the poaching liquid. Cover the saucepan with a tight lid and cook dumplings for about 25 minutes. Then, check if the balls are firm if not cook further for a while. Then, remove the lid from the pan, and cook for five minutes more, so that the liquid evaporates and the balls golden.

10. Pour the Vanilla sauce and devour!

26. The German Radler

This traditional German drink has an interesting story behind its making. The word "Radler" means cyclists. A few cyclists on their trip in Bavaria had mixed German lager with lemon juice due to the shortage of beer. So, this drink was named Radler. This drink is mostly made with lager mixed with lemonade or lemon soda. It is refreshing with a balanced taste. So, let us see the easy steps of making it.

Serving Size: 1
Preparation Time: 2 Minutes
Ingredients:

- 1 Part lager
- 1 Part lemon soda, Iced cold

Instructions:
1. Fill half of a glass with iced lemon soda.
2. Pour in beer and fill the rest of the glass with it.
3. Serve Immediately!

27. Extra Delicious German Pretzels

These German pretzels are a good idea for a unique treat. They have a unique fancy shape to delight you already. These soft and delicious pretzels are perfect for snacks. You can serve them with sauce or hummus and can also store them for up to three days. You will also find a few tricks in the recipe to bring the authentic and traditional German taste to it. So, let us go through some easy steps of making it.

Serving Size: 12

Preparation Time: 25 Minutes

Cooking Time: 15 Minutes

Ingredients:

- 9 cups Water
- 4 Cups All-purpose Flour
- 1 ½ Cups Lukewarm water
- ½ Cup Baking Soda
- 1 tbsp Unsalted Butter, melted
- 1 tbsp Brown sugar
- 2¼ tsp Instant or Dry yeast
- 1 tsp salt
- Coarse sea salt

Instructions:

1. In a bowl, add the lukewarm water and mix the yeast. Set aside for one minute.

2. Now, add to it the butter, brown sugar, and salt. Whisk to combine.

3. Add three cups of all-purpose flour, one cup at a time. Attach the dough hook to the mixer or knead with your hands until a soft and bouncy dough form. You can add more flour if the dough is sticky and knead again.

4. Knead the dough on a lightly floured surface and form a ball. Cover the dough ball with a paper towel or wrap and set aside for about ten minutes.

5. Preheat your oven to 400° Fahrenheit and line baking sheets with silicone baking mats.

6. Cut the dough into 1/3 cup portions.

7. Now, make around 20-inches rope. Draw the ends together like a circle and twirl, bringing towards you. Attach like the pretzels shown in the image.

8. In a large pot, add about nine cups of water with baking soda and bring it to boil. Now, place your pretzel sticks in it, few at a time. Cook for only about twenty to thirty seconds and remove using a slotted spoon. Drain the excess water. Cooking for more time can destroy the taste.

9. Now, arrange the pretzels on the baking sheets prepared with silicon paper mats.

10. Repeat the same steps for all pretzels.

11. Bake the pretzels in the preheated oven for about twelve to fifteen minutes until golden.

12. Serve hot with hummus, mustard, or nacho cheese sauce.

28. The Traditional Maultaschen

If you are looking for devouring food, this traditional German Maultaschen is for you. It is a pocket of seasoned ground burger with a dressing of stock. You can choose any stock or broth you like. This Maultaschen is as tasty as it is fancy and as fulfilling as it sounds. So, let us go through the steps of making this fulfilling dish.

Serving Size: 6
Preparation Time: 1 Hour
Cooking Time: 25 Minutes
Ingredients:

- ¼ lb. Ground Burger
- 4 Eggs
- 3 Bacon Strips, Chopped and cooked
- 2.5 oz Spinach
- 6 Cups broth or stock
- 2 Cups Flour
- 3 Green Onions, Chopped

- I Onion, diced
- 2 tbsp heavy cream
- 2 tbsp breadcrumbs (Italian style)
- I tbsp Olive oil
- ½ tsp dried parsley
- ½ tsp Nutmeg
- Salt to taste
- Pepper to taste

Instructions:

1. In a mixing bowl, add the flour, three eggs, a teaspoon of salt, and olive oil. Place the dough hook to the mixer and mix until smooth for about ten minutes.

2. When ready, wrap the dough with a plastic wrapper and refrigerate it for about thirty minutes.

3. Now, in a pot, bring water to boil over high heat and add the spinach in it.

4. Cook for three minutes and then rinse in cold water. Drain and dice once cool.

5. Heat a pan and add the ground burger. Cook until brown. Add the one diced onion to it when the ground burger has half done.

6. When it has almost done, add the spinach, nutmeg, parsley, breadcrumbs, and the cream.

7. Stir to mix the ingredients and cook until the ground burger is cook through.

8. When done, transfer the mixture to the refrigerator until needed.

9. Now, take the dough out and roll it out on a clean and

lightly floured surface until very thin. Cut 3 x 5-inch sheets of even number.

10. Take the filling out from the fridge and add the remaining egg in a small bowl.

11. Place a little portion on one sheet of the dough. Brush the edges of the sheet with egg wash and place another sheet on the top. Press the edges with your fingers or a fork to crimp.

12. Repeat similar steps for making remaining Maultaschen.

13. Bring water to boil in a large pot for cooking Maultaschen.

14. Carefully add the Maultaschen to it and cook for about ten minutes

15. Warm the broth or stock and place it in a bowl.

16. Now, place the cooked Maultaschen in the stock bowl.

17. Garnish with chopped green onions and serve!

29. The Hearty German Meatballs with Sauerkraut

If you are a German food lover, you should try this flavorful dish. This fulfilling dish is a traditional German recipe and is usually served with a special white sauce. The sauce made of Sauerkraut adds flavors to it and also gives it a fancy look. This combination of meatballs is widely popular and is now ready to devour you. So, let us see the steps of making it.

Serving Size: 6

Preparation Time: 50 minutes

Cooking Time: 25 minutes (5 Days for fermenting sauerkraut sauce, if preparing at home)

Ingredients:

- ½ lb. ground pork
- 4 1/2 lb. pale green or white cabbage, cored
- 1 lb. ground beef
- ¾ cup fine breadcrumbs dry
- ½ cup finely chopped onion
- 1 tbsp fresh parsley snipped
- ½ cup 2% milk
- 1 Large egg, beaten
- ½ cup water, optional
- 3 tbsp coarse crystal sea salt
- 2 to 3 tbsp vegetable oil
- 1-1/2 tsp salt
- 1 tsp of caraway seeds
- 1 tsp of Worcestershire sauce
- 1 tsp peppercorns
- 1/8 tsp pepper
- Additional snipped parsley

Instructions:

1. Take a large bowl and into it add beef, onion, pork,

parsley, breadcrumbs, salt, pepper, Worcestershire sauce, beaten eggs, and milk. Mix them well and shape the mixture into 18 meatballs.

2. Onto a skillet, heat the oil and brown the prepared meatballs. When done, remove them from the skillet, and drain the fast from them.

3. To prepare the sauerkraut sauce, thoroughly wash a large bowl. Now, rinse the bowl with boiling water. Keep all the ingredients and equipments you are going to use for Cabbage clean.

4. Use a container that is clean and big enough to fit all the cabbage comfortably, leaving few inches of space from the top.

5. Finely shred the cabbage and layer it along with the salt in the bowl.

6. Massage the cabbage along with salt for about 5 minutes, then wait for 5 minutes and then repeat. In the end, the total volume of cabbage should reduce.

7. Add the caraway seeds and peppercorns into the bowl.

8. Covering its surface with cling film sheet, squeeze out all the air bubbles. Using a few heavy plates, weigh down the cabbage and cover it as much as possible. Brines' level would rise a little while covering the cabbage.

9. Now, cover the bowl and place it in a dark place with cool temperature for minimum of five days. Ferment for about two to six weeks for maximum flavor.

10. Keep checking the cabbage once in a day to see if any gas releases have built up while fermenting, stirring it to release the bubbles. Remove scum if formed on the cabbage. Then rinse the weights again in the boiling water, and cover

with a new cling film. Foam should appear by now on the top of the brine and bubbles inside the cabbage. Keep the cabbage at even and cool temperatures to get the perfect results.

11. Now, spoon the prepared sauerkraut into the skillet and top it with meatballs.

12. Cover the skillet and add to it the meatball and sauerkraut mixture. Simmer for about 15-20 minutes or till the meatballs are cooked through. Then, add more water if necessary. When done, serve hot and garnish with parsley.

30. The German Traditional Cheesecake

The combination of cheese and cake in itself is delectable. This Cheesecake is a traditional German recipe that you can make without having any culinary experience. This cake is oozing with the flavor of the cheese. It has a great taste and is soft with a beautiful texture. You can enjoy this cake with your friends and see it vanish in a few seconds. Now, let me first share the steps of making this delicious Cheesecake.

Serving Size: 12

Preparation Time: 20 Minutes

Cooking Time: 5 hours 10 Minutes

Ingredients:

- 1 lb. curd cottage cheese or quark
- 3 tbsp All-Purpose Flour
- 8 oz Cream Cheese, softened
- 1 ½ Cups White Sugar
- 4 Eggs
- ½ Cup softened Butter
- 2 tbsp Corn starch
- 1 tsp Vanilla extract
- 1 tbsp Lemon juice
- 1 ½ tsp lemon juice

Instructions:

1. Preheat your oven to 350° Fahrenheit and grease a nine-inch spring form pan.

2. In a bowl, combine the flour, sugar, and corn starch. Mix well and set aside.

3. Now, in a mixing bowl, add both the cheeses and beat until fluffy using a mixer or food processor.

4. Add the butter to it and beat again.

5. Now, add the flour mixture to it and mix again to combine. Then add eggs, one by one. Blend well and add the lemon juice and vanilla extract. Mix well.

6. Now, transfer the mixture to the greased pan. Bake the cake for an hour and ten minutes.

7. When done, let it rest in the oven for about two hours and then refrigerate for another four hours.

8. Slice and Enjoy!

CONCLUSION

Congrats! We have reached the end of this book. I hope you have explored a new world of cooking with this book, and it has helped you add to your skills. Apart from many methods of cooking, you must now have learned about various tricks to make your food extra-delicious.

More importantly, I hope you enjoy the process of cooking and have made some great memories while cooking. These memories and the experiences are going to stay with you forever and going to build as you cook more. So, do not stop cooking and devouring yourself!

Guten Appetit!